This book belongs to:

....

A Bowyer Book
Published in the United Kingdom
by Bowyer Publishing in 2018
Copyright © Paquita Lamacraft
All rights reserved
The moral right of the author has been asserted.

No part of this book may be reproduced, stored in a retrieval system, or transmitted in any form or by any means without the prior written consent of the publisher, nor reproduced, circulated in any manner in any form or binding other than that in which it is published and without a similar condition including this condition being imposed on the subsequent purchaser. The only exception is a reviewer who may publish short excerpts in a published review. Commercialised book summaries are expressly prohibited and unauthorised unless specifically licensed by the publisher.

This book is presented for information and entertainment purposes only. The information presented herein represents the view of the author at date of publication. The author reserves the right to alter and update opinions based on new information and new conditions. While every attempt has been made to verify the information in this book, neither the author nor affiliates/partners assume any responsibility for errors, inaccuracies, or omissions. At no time can any of the information herein be construed as professional, investment, tax, accounting, or legal advice, nor does it constitute a recommendation or warrant of suitability for any particular business, industry, transaction, or business strategy.

ISBN: 978-1-9996273-3-1

Author's Web Address: www.paquitalamacraft.com
Bowyer Publishing- A Division of Archer Business Group
PO Box 666, Eastleigh, Hampshire, England SO50 0PA

Dancing takes you to places you would not otherwise go – and so it was that I was first introduced to Cuba.

On my first trip I discovered a passion in dance that I had not encountered before, and met Cuban friends of Australian friends who had been working there advising on methods of permaculture.

Permaculture is an environmentally powerful form of using nature to increase yield and sustainability in farming and was pioneered by two Australians, Bill Mollison and David Holmgren. Their principles have had influenced across the globe. I reference them at the back of the book because they form a useful parallel guide to the art of letting go.

At the time of my first visit one of our dancing friends knew some of the Australian permaculture instructor team then working close to Havana. The time spent with them was one of the door openers for my view of a Cuba that varies from that we usually see as a tourist.

The other door – and it proved the most enduring – was through the eyes of friends we had made ourselves, the most influential being the one whom I call Nemo in the book The Cuban Approach. Sadly, I couldn't find Nemo (hence the nickname) on my No Plan visit.

Cuba is a fascinating place and sufficiently removed from so many of the social expectations that influence our lives in a western culture. These cause you to challenge your own thinking on things of which you were previously certain.

By the time I made the trip of this book it had been many years since I had been there before. Nothing much had changed. But this time I had a whole month at my leisure and was determined to travel outside Havana and experience some of the life of my Cuban friends.

The trip had effects that caught me unawares.

Removed from the impact of daily communications from my usual world my subconscious had the space and opportunity to bring to the experiences of my travel particular vignettes from my past.

Many were painful events that thought I had dealt with. Obviously not.

Many were flashbacks to childhood, to friendships or to other travels. They warmed my soul with their colourful memories.

Many came from experiencing another reality far less fortunate than mine.

Each of these things has had a long lasting effect on my life for it taught me the fine art of letting go.

The quotes here come from the book of my one month with no plan travels in the countryside of Cuba.

Some are my own and others are from others who have thought about the elements of the fine art of letting go.

> Each reflects the lessons I learned.

> Perhaps they ring home to you too.

I hope you enjoy the quotes I use to illustrate the trip and after reading this little book emerge at the end smiling, thoughtful, refreshed, renewed and with new hope for the future you are capable of achieving – if only you practice the art of letting go.

Paquita

"There is a time for action and a time to let the winds direction become known.

The Cuban Approach is to make the most of the moments in between."

Paquita Lamacraft
From the Book 'The Cuban Approach'

> *"Perhaps we try too hard to control our fate.*
>
> *With a focus on control we forget to read the tides and so lose the chance to raise our sails to catch the best winds to ride them."*

Paquita Lamacraft
From the Book 'The Cuban Approach'

"Friends:
- *Keep you honest.*
- *Pull you up when you are out of order: They can because you know they love you anyway.*
- *Give you an uncluttered mirror in which to review your own actions as well as see those of others from a perspective different from yours.*
- *Remind you who you are when you have temporarily lost your way."*

Paquita Lamacraft
From the Book 'The Cuban Approach'

*"All human beings should try
to learn
before they die
what they are running from,
and to,
and why."*

James Thurber

James Thurber was a much loved writer and humourist who had the art of caricaturing the foibles of us all. His plays 'The Male Animal' and 'The Secret Life of Walter Mitty' were adapted to award winning films and his cartoons and short stories are rich contributions to American literature.

Becoming night blind from cataracts, Thurber once wrote that he felt only the half blind see the world creatively. In 'The Admiral at the Wheel' he revealed why: "The Cuban Flag over a national bank becomes an American flag, the gay old lady with a gray parasol walking right through the side of a truck was a garbage man with a garbage can on his back, the cat that rolled across the street like a striped barrel was just a piece of butcher's paper blowing in the wind, and the floating bridges, smoke from tugs hanging in the wind."

Impaired by sight but never by imagination, his works endure – for the value of his cartoons and his great wit and skill in writing.

> *"If you find people untrustworthy you had better look in the mirror instead of through the window."*

Paquita Lamacraft
From the Book 'The Cuban Approach'

*"Don't lower your sails
when you have no sense of
direction.*

*Opportunity brings its own
direction.*

*If you lower your sails
you have announced to the
universe
that you don't expect to be
able to catch the next wind."*

Paquita Lamacraft
From the Book 'The Cuban Approach'

"We require from buildings two kinds of goodness:

first, the doing their practical duty well, then, that they be graceful and pleasing in doing it."

John Ruskin

John Ruskin was a Victorian polymath, art critic and patron, draughtsman, watercolourist and social activist.

His interests and writing include subjects as diverse as architecture, geology, myth, botany, ornithology, education and political economics.

The many and extensive family continental travels of his youth, and later as an adult, perhaps form the basis of this quotation – for he was a great observer of detail and critic of what he saw to be unaligned with grace of line and adequacy of function.

"If you fear losing your way remember that your only obligation in this life is to be true to yourself.

This is the compass that keeps you aligned to true north.

If you use this compass you will never go far off course."

Paquita Lamacraft
From the Book 'The Cuban Approach'

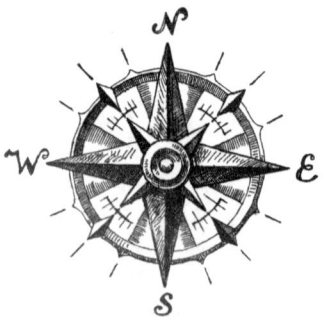

"Sometimes, the best healing takes place in years distant from events and in places geographically unconnected to the circumstance of the cause of the hurt."

Paquita Lamacraft
From the Book 'The Cuban Approach'

"Safety is not just the responsibility of the company where you work:

it's yours – and you ignore it at your peril."

Philip Smallman

Outdoorsman, adventurer and tree surgeon, Philip Smallman was embarking on a career as a noted teacher of his profession. He loves trees and had just started to develop a career as a public speaker advocating careful practice. His watch phrase was: 'Make every cut your hallmark'.

That was before he was made paraplegic by a fall caused by mismatch in his equipment. He had read about some issues but thought they didn't apply to him as he was always very careful.

Rather than let his new disability deter him from his passions, Phil took up flying and became a wheelchair tennis champion. He travelled outback to spend time with his former friends in aboriginal communities, adapting equipment as he went.

Needing to find a new way to make a living he took the lessons he learned too late to be the basis of his business. He now speaks to groups – especially in big manufacturing plants – to make the safety message personal. He is a charismatic, charming person and when he speaks you can almost hear the silence. The emotional response to his talk and interaction with his audience can be seen on every face. It leaves a searing memory.

Despite repeated and lucrative offers to film his talks, Phil has always refused. He knows the impact of his presence has a far deeper impact. He is a remarkable person.

> *"You get comfortable with some mindsets: they come to feel more like facts than opinions."*

Paquita Lamacraft
From the Book 'The Cuban Approach'

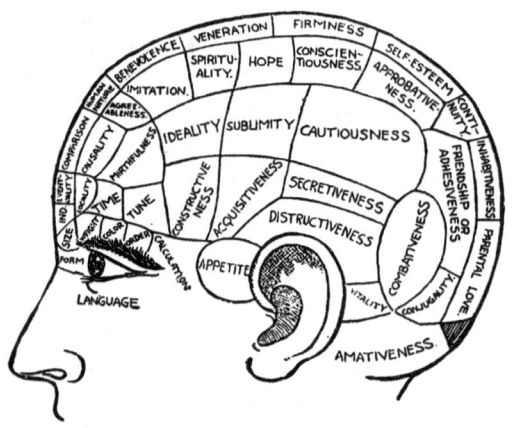

*"Sometimes we need to have
a reality shock
to adjust our viewpoints and
expectations.*

*When they happen,
these reality shocks
cause our views to be
readjusted
more substantially than we
ever expected."*

Paquita Lamacraft
From the Book 'The Cuban Approach'

"What is life, if full of care we have no time to stand and stare."

W.H. Auden

Born in York, England, Wystan Hugh Auden studied literature at Christ Church, Oxford before becoming an established writer.

His works included not just the poems for which he is probably most remembered, but also operatic plays, documentary films, and writings on diverse subjects of social importance.

Having witnessed the Spanish Civil War he was greatly moved by the suffering it wrought and he felt that to be an effective poet a person should also be something of a journalist.

Perhaps that is why he moves us, for he touches the reality of our emotions and of life.

"Detours teach you a lot about yourself

*and when you rejoin the main road
it is never the same
as before."*

Paquita Lamacraft
From the Book 'The Cuban Approach'

"The wind brings on it both dreams and specks that can get in your eye.

Dream your dreams and set your sails.

A speck in the eye is a small price to pay."

Paquita Lamacraft
From the Book 'The Cuban Approach'

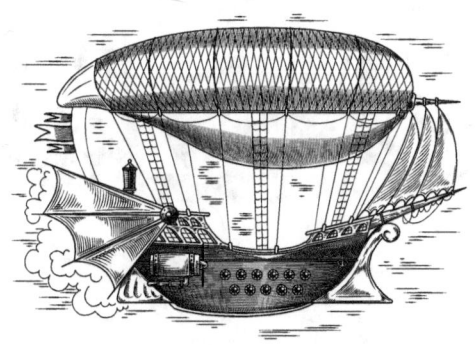

"An unhurried sense of time is in itself a form of wealth."

Bonnie Freedman

Canadian lawyer Bonnie Freedman leads the regional practice of Privacy and Data Protection of Borden Ladner Gervais LLP in Toronto. She has been active as a leader in her profession in informing the development of laws in this evolving area of jurisprudence.

As she says, it is a fascinating and evolving subject area. There is no common application able to be made, as each case needs to consider the sometimes complex perspective of all parties involved. In an interview with the Law Times she commented that this means that to be able to 'keep up': "You don't sleep a lot and you read a lot".

We can all associate with her appreciation of how precious are the moments of unhurried time.

*"Chance is always powerful.
Let your hook always be cast.
In the pool where you least expect it,
there will be fish."*

Ovid

Publius Ovidius Naso is known to us simpy as Ovid. He lived in the reign of Augustus and was a contemporary of both Horace and Virgil. Although a much revered poet of his time, he was later exiled in 8 AD to Tomis, the ancient but remote Black Sea settlement now known as the Romanian port city of Constanța. He died in exile.

In 2017 Rome City Council formally followed Florence (2008) and his home town of Sulmona in acquitting Ovid of any wrong doing. The cause of his exile was not documented and has long been a subject of conjecture: his overly erotic verse, his dislike of Augustus, or perhaps something else. This restoration of a famous son shows the respect due to his works that has weathered the centuries.

Ovid's 15-book continous mythological epic 'Metamorphoses' is one of the most important sources of classical mythology. His whole range of works, including his elegiac couplets, has long been an influence on Western art and literature.

*"The wind around one island
– though it be the
same wind –*

*might be harnessed
differently
to give a different outcome."*

Paquita Lamacraft
From the Book 'The Cuban Approach'

"In the middle of the least prepossessing circumstances there is often beauty to be found."

Paquita Lamacraft
From the Book 'The Cuban Approach'

*"A cucumber is bitter.
Throw it away.
There are briars in the road.
Turn aside from them.*

*This is enough.
Do not add,
...and why were such things
made in the world?"*

Marcus Aurelius

Marcus Aurelias is known as the 'Philosopher Emperor' of Rome, ruling from 161 to 180. He found the contrast between his Stoic philosophy and the demands of court life challenging. His 12 book 'Meditations', which was written for himself and not for wider distribution, reveals thoughts on self-management to retain honour. In it he writes that one should ponder one's place in the universe, and that as everything came from nature so will everything return.

He would only reign together with his adoptive brother Lucius Verus and it was the only time Rome had two Caesars. He reigned successfully to quell insurrection on many fronts of the empire and it is generally agreed that his death marked the end of the Pax Romana. This was a period of relative stability and peace during which the Roman Empire ruled a third of the world's population. It lasted some 206 years.

Ovid's legacy has been longer, influencing the works of future writers including Chaucer, Shakespeare, Dante, and Milton.

"Free always has a catch. Free can be very expensive."

Paquita Lamacraft
From the Book 'The Cuban Approach'

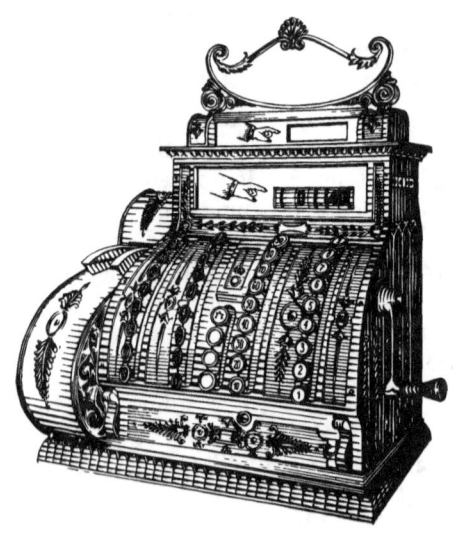

"Hope is a mysterious thing. It keeps us going against awful odds."

Paquita Lamacraft
From the Book 'The Cuban Approach'

"The only way to know whether to trust someone is to trust someone."

Ernest Hemingway

An Illinois boy, Ernest Hemingway went on to lead a life played out in the full spectrum of vibrancy of the Spanish Civil War, the lively Paris of the 1920s, Cuba, China (which he didn't like), on safari in Africa where he survived (but with debilitating pain thereafter) two plane crashes, and through his four marriages. He was present at the Normandy landings and the liberation of Paris.

A journalist, war correspondent, and author of many plays that have been made into films including 'The Sun Also Rises' and 'For Whom the Bell Tolls'. He won the Pulitzer Prize in 1953 for 'The Old Man and the Sea'. His acceptance speech summarised the inner life of a writer: "Writing, at its best, is a lonely life".

In 1954 he won the Nobel Prize for literature for the same book. The medal he gifted to the Cuban people by leaving it in the care of the patron saint of Cuba, the Virgin de Cobre.

After electroshock treatments at the Mayo Clinic to treat his depression, Hemingway committed suicide by shooting himself in the head. His works live on to inspire us.

> *"Fishing is a chance to be alone with just yourself – and possibly catch fish."*

Paquita Lamacraft
From the Book 'The Cuban Approach'

"Sometimes you need to make your own detours.

'Around' is often the quickest way through."

Paquita Lamacraft
From the Book 'The Cuban Approach'

"The secret of architectural excellence is to translate the proportions of a dachshund into bricks, mortar, and marble."

Christopher Wren

We know Christopher Wren for his famous architectural works: following the Great Fire of London, those of St. Paul's Cathedral and his 51 new churches, plus Trinity College Library and the chapel for Pembroke College Cambridge, the Sheldonian Theatre in Oxford, The Royal Observatory, and the facade at Hampton Court Palace.

However like many of his time, Wren had interests across many disciplines. He studied mathematics and engineering and was an inventor, creating an instrument for writing in the dark and a pneumatic machine. He was also a professor of astronomy and one of the founding members of the Royal Society.

Elegance of scale is his mark. As the inscription on his gravestone in Westminster Abbey says when translated from the Latin: 'If you seek his memorial, look about you'.

*"Depending on how you view something,
your conclusions can be coloured by your own expectations
and then you see what you think you see
rather than what you do."*

Paquita Lamacraft
From the Book 'The Cuban Approach'

"Often the most rewarding things are those that at first glance seem inconsequential but later mark out that moment as special."

Paquita Lamacraft
From the Book 'The Cuban Approach'

*" To be nobody-but-yourself
in a world which is doing
its best,
night and day,
to make you everybody else
—
means to fight the hardest
battle
which any human being can
fight;
and never stop fighting."*

e.e. cummings

Edward Estlin Cummings (e.e.) is said to be the only person to make avante garde writing popular with readers.

Experimenting with words and their placement on the page, Cummings often made new words by combination of two existing words or changing endings to give new meaning. His word placement is a typographical poem in itself. He decided on his vocation at an early age and thereafter between the ages of eight and twenty-two he wrote a poem a day.

He was a great love poet but his works also reflect the period of internment he suffered while an ambulance driver during WWI in France. He was suspected of treason as a result of befriending soldiers of nearby units, but eventually released.

Cummings believed that poetry was a 'process' and not a 'product'.

For many, such as this author who discovered his work while studying English Literature at Sydney University, his poems were, and continue to be a magical insight into the possibilities of words.

*"Trust in God
but row away from
the rocks."*

Breton Fishermen's saying

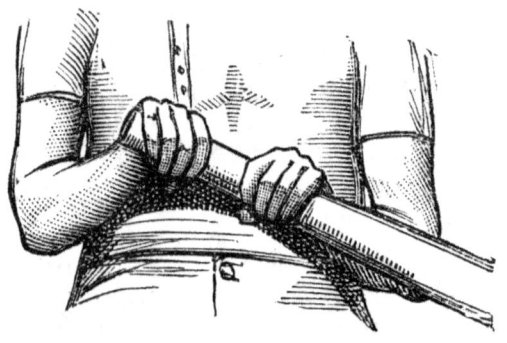

"Live your own life: not mine."

Seen on a bumper sticker on a bus in Ceinfuegos

"Imitation is the sincerest flattery."

George Caleb Cotton

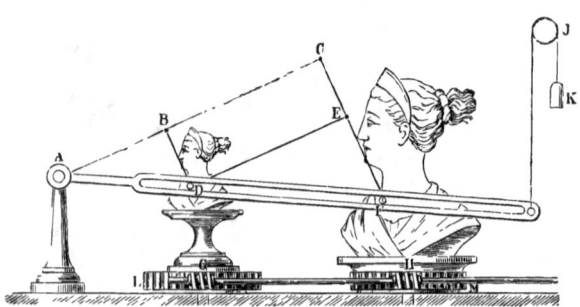

George Caleb Cotton was an Anglican parish priest administering to the early settlers of Saint-Armand, Quebec.

He lived as the locals lived until he could gain a church and patronage. That meant boarding with eight other people in a two roomed cabin for four years.

He farmed and cleared three homesteads and was disappointed to not receive the posting to Toronto for which he had been proposed.

A man of frail health, apparently unremarkable wit, but pious and with the habit of plain speech sometimes untarnished by diplomacy, Cotton served his congregation for 40 years.

"Computers make it easier to do a lot of things, but most of the things they make it easier to do don't need to be done."

Andy Rooney

Andy Rooney was a much loved American journalist, news and current affairs correspondent, social commentator, wit and former war correspondent. He became an American institution and spent a lifetime entertaining us with his acerbic comments that always provoked thoughtfulness as well as a smile.

Rooney was one of the first journalists to visit the concentration camps when writing for Stars and Stripes and said that it changed his views on war forever. Previously a pacifist, he felt after this experience that there was no such thing as a 'just war'. In his post war correspondent years he complained about everything from shoelaces, coffee cans, eyebrows, pill bottles and the gifts that people kept sending him.

Formerly calling himself an agnostic he later claimed to be an atheist. In the classic 60 Minutes segment about those gifts he explained that as a result he had been sent many Bibles and copies of the Quran. He said that he had read them both extensively and had come to the conclusion that one was definitely better than the other.

It was typical commentary from someone whose style was unique.

*"There is always the type of
place you want
at the price you can afford.

You just have to find it."*

Paquita Lamacraft
From the Book 'The Cuban Approach'

"Invitation pre-requisites:

- *Must demonstrate generosity of spirit*
- *Not take self too seriously*
- *Have a sense of occasion."*

Paquita Lamacraft
From the Book 'The Cuban Approach'

"Don't tell fish stories where the people know you; but particularly, don't tell them where they know the fish."

Mark Twain

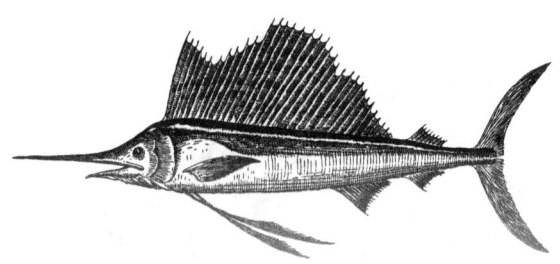

Samuel L. Clemens, who wrote under the pen name of Mark Twain, became one of the most celebrated of American writers, famous around the world. His novels 'Adventures of Huckleberry Finn' and 'The Adventures of Tom Sawyer' are to this day, classics.

'Huckleberry Finn' was the first time that the voice of the common man speaking in the vernacular was heard in a novel. In it, Twain draws the colour, excitement, meanness and criminal violence that characterised river towns in the era.

Twain rose from abject poverty when his unsmiling father died and his lively, fun-loving and tender-hearted mother struggled to even feed the family. His first job at the age of 12 was as an apprenticed printer, but he eventually achieved his dream of becoming a qualified riverboat captain until all civilian river traffic ceased in the Civil War. His pseudonym reflects that heritage: 'Mark Twain' is steamboat slang for '12 feet of water'.

His funny, irreverent and often satirical writing style was always able to deflate the pretentious.

"In life, seize the moment and relish its delight.

We never know what the future may bring but we can be in control of the moment."

Paquita Lamacraft
From the Book 'The Cuban Approach'

*"The invisible thread that
binds you
to those you care about
is stronger than fibre optics."*

Paquita Lamacraft
From the Book 'The Cuban Approach'

*"Know when to hold 'em,
know when to fold 'em,
know when to walk away
and when to run."*

Willie Nelson

Enduring, talented, and with an immediately identifiable voice, Willie Nelson has been singing and playing guitar since he was a youngster. His first song was written at age 7 and he joined his first band at 10.

Nelson has sung with and written for most of the legendary country singers of this era and when his assets were seized by the IRS to collect on $32 million of taxes estimated to be due, help was forthcoming. With incapacity to pay and all his future revenue claimed by the IRS until the debt was cleared, Nelson released 'The IRS tape: Who will buy my memories?'

Nelson had supported the farmers with Farm Aid and now they gave back. His enthusiastic support from fans cleared the debt which had been negotiated down. Many bought his assets and donated or rented them back to him for a low price. Nelson later sued Price Waterhouse for their management of his funds and the case was settled out of court.

Not always known is that at the same time his fans delivered on a promise to his daughter to buy her dream ranch. They bought it on his behalf so it was out of the scope of IRS rulings.

Willie Nelson's songs are globally loved. Their lyrical expression of the human condition moves even those who don't care much for country music.

"Hope is not a method."

General Gordon Sullivan

General Sullivan may have been the last person his classmates expected to rise to become the 32nd Army Chief of Staff. He came from humble roots and was a scholarship student who worked as a waiter and a construction worker to pay his way.

Together with military strategist Colonel Michael Harper, Sullivan redesigned an underfunded, bureaucracy-bound military to become an effective purpose-designed force fit for the information age.

His leadership by example and his personal approach to empowering his own leaders gives valuable lessons for all who face structuring outmoded arrangements to meet new challenges.

Demanding high standards of himself and those whom he leads, General Sullivan embodies all that is best in military behaviour and human interactions to develop the best in others. His hallmark seems to be his ability to be honest, fun-loving, focused and with great empathy. He has the ability to encourage the best from everyone – military and civilian. His care was equal to the soldiers who served, as to their families.

One of his telling comments was "The Army isn't about soldiers: It is soldiers".

"Imitation and improvisation together can create an original whose value is doubled by its story."

Paquita Lamacraft
From the Book 'The Cuban Approach'

"The end is possibly not the end.

*What is important
is that you live while you live,
and you feel all
that is good and positive
before you die."*

Paquita Lamacraft
From the Book 'The Cuban Approach'

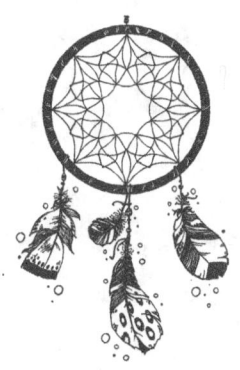

"We owe something to extravagance, for thrift and adventure seldom go hand in hand."

Jennie Churchill

Jennie Churchill knew something about extravagance. Daughter of a wealthy New York financier, she met her future husband by being introduced by the Prince of Wales, (later to become King Edward VII) at a sailing regatta on the Isle of Wight. Three months later the 20 year old beauty was married to Lord Randolph Churchill.

Eight months later, she was to give to birth to their first son, Winston, the future Prime Minister of England.

Intelligent, witty and an accomplished pianist, she was quick to laugh and reputedly great company as well as having striking good looks.

After Randolph's death at age 45 Jennie went on to mix in the highest and wealthiest social circles, marrying first George Cornwallis-West (26 days older than Winston) and then Montagu Phippen Porch (younger than Winston by three years) who was serving in Nigeria as a British Civil Servant, later to become a successful businessman.

When they married Jennie memorably said: "He has a future and I have a past, so we should be alright."

*"One man's delay
is another man's
good fortune."*

Paquita Lamacraft
From the Book 'The Cuban Approach'

"The way things are is the way things are."

Paquita Lamacraft
From the Book 'The Cuban Approach'

"If your heart is a volcano, how do you expect the flowers to bloom?"

Kahlil Gibran

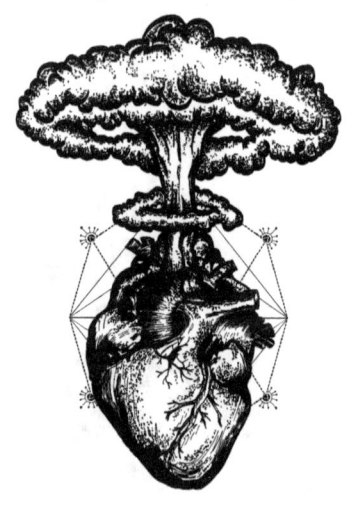

Gibran Khalil Gibran was a Lebanese-American writer, poet, visual artist and Syrian nationalist. His book 'The Prophet' had a cool critical reception but sold well. In fact he follows Shakespeare and Laozi to be the third-best-selling poet of all time.

His mystical philosophy was based on spiritual love and is seen as a convergence of Christianity, Islam, Judaism, and Theosophy. He expressed it this way: "You are my brother and I love you. I love you when you prostrate yourself in your mosque, and kneel in your church and pray in your synagogue. You and I are sons of one faith—the Spirit."

Gibran's home town of Bsharri sits over 3,000 metres above sea level and is a famous ski resort and home to the last cedars of Lebanon. It is here that Gibran wished to be buried. Next to his grave is inscribed: "I am alive like you, and I am standing beside you. Close your eyes and look around, you will see me in front of you."

"Those of us who travel to seek the soul of a place understand that time spent waiting is not lost."

Paquita Lamacraft
From the Book 'The Cuban Approach'

*"The things that sear our
hearts the deepest
never truly heal.*

*You get used to the hurt
but it remains somewhere
in your soul."*

Paquita Lamacraft
From the Book 'The Cuban Approach'

"Make every fault a fashion."

Fiona Lamacraft

Funny, witty, thoughtful and creative, my mother, Fiona, was a remarkable example of the ability to make the best of whatever the situation demanded. From bits of this and that she could make a home as gracious as those of her very wealthy forebears.

She survived polio, the first global Asian Flu Epidemic, and cancer – and until her death encouraged everyone around her to shine, to trust, to be the best version of themselves they could be.

When I spilled red wine on a favourite yellow outfit she exemplified this quote by suggesting I paint a daisy over it. I had just flown in for a day or so and had no alternative clothes before flying back to join my partner on the last leg home after an overseas trip. This outfit had been especially chosen as it matched the yellow sapphire I had just received from him as an engagement ring.

My daisies were a great success, and Fiona's kindness and wisdom lives on in the memories of many.

"Set your course by the stars, not by the lights of every passing ship."

Old Navy saying

When my partner, my mother and then my Dad died in less than 14 months of each other I was deeply challenged by the fact that my whole world had changed forever.

Following my father's death I asked myself: "Where is the plus side of all this?"

It took a while to find it.

The plus side was that I now had no obligations to anyone in life. I could define my own direction.

   I did.

      It has been a wonderful adventure.

         It hasn't been easy

            Life generally isn't.

But I would have missed so much if I had been mired in negatives.

The key was practicing the art of letting go.

The Cuban Approach employs fifteen principles to give new perspectives on life and yourself.

1. Speak your dreams into existence.
2. Plan ahead but carry your lifeboat with you.
3. You can be lost without feeling lost.
4. Trust your judgment – and then trust in others.
5. Be kind.
6. Challenge your mindsets.
7. Some of the best memories have no photograph.
8. Rough terrain is best crossed in good company.
9. The way things are is the way things are.
10. A smile is a universal bridge.
11. Time doing nothing is well invested
12. Perspective is not just for artists to learn.
13. The quickest way through is often around.
14. If you give of yourself you give twice.
15. Sometimes you are somewhere not for your benefit – but for the benefit of others.

Permaculture is based on 12 principles in designing the best agricultural opportunities offered by a particular piece of land.

Its rules as I apply them to life may guide you to plant and reap and grow and enjoy the contours of your corner of this world .

May you reap a better harvest and relish the experience as you practice the art of letting go.

1. Observe and interact
2. Catch and store energy
3. Obtain a yield
4. Apply self-regulation and feedback
5. Use and value renewable resources and services
6. Produce no waste
7. Design from nature's patterns and then fill in detail
8. Integrate rather than segregate
9. Use small and slow solutions
10. Use and value diversity
11. Use edges and value the marginal
12. Creatively use and respond to change

These aren't bad rules for life and practicing the art of letting go.

1. Observe and interact

Taking your hurt, anger and self-consciousness into hiding only gives it a dark place to grow. If you take yourself to where you can interact with nature, it has a healing effect on your soul and you return refreshed and more positive.

2. Catch and store energy

A lot of what we do is just rushing about. A lot of worrying we do is about things that might never happen. Save your energy. Put positives in place of your worries.

Don't underestimate the power of taking the time to 'stand and stare'.

3. Obtain a yield

What is consuming your energy, your goodwill, your time and your cheerfulness? It is worth expending all of these – or any of them – but only if they are generating some result.

One example may be displaying tough love. It can return more than making excuses for behaviour that you shouldn't excuse. Instead nudge towards the honesty of taking individual responsibility for life and not blaming anyone or anything.

4. Apply self-regulation & feedback

We all have developed mindsets that are worth challenging. When we realise that what we see as a Must Do may just be the way we are used to seeing something – and possibly not the best way – it's worth rethinking. Perhaps the things about which we are the most definite can benefit from being reconsidered.

5. Use and value renewable resources and services

Value your friends and family and your pets – they are what give your life meaning. It can be easy to forget to show how much you appreciate them.

6. Produce no waste

What you do in life should have some meaning so you leave the world with better things and not the things that are easily tossed aside as just 'filling in time'.

7. Design from nature's patterns and then fill in detail

Everywhere there is beauty to be seen and lessons to be learned. Each offers something personal to the individual.

They are found when we have the quiet time for them to surface to our conscious thoughts.

If you are connected to something electronic all the time they have no chance to do so.

8. Integrate rather than segregate
Take the thinking of Abraham Lincoln to heart when he mused to himself:

> "I don't like that man.
> I must get to know him better."

9. Use small and slow solutions
Letting go isn't a one off event. It is a way of thinking. Changing habits takes time. Reward yourself for each small step you make in practicing the art of letting go.

10. Use and value diversity
Even the way you stack the dishwasher can benefit from another perspective.

The way you do things may not be the way of another but their way is no less valid than yours.

11. Use edges and value the marginal
Sometimes the real value is found not in the blaringly obvious but in the small things that make memorable moments and with the small kindnesses that have disproportionately great impact.

Sometimes people you least think have something to offer just haven't ever had the opportunity to express their thoughts.

12. Creatively use and respond to change
Change is never easy, but if we look for the positive it's always there.

www.ingramcontent.com/pod-product-compliance
Lightning Source LLC
Chambersburg PA
CBHW050042080526
44586CB00014B/1423